50 Delightful Tea-Time Treats

By: Kelly Johnson

Table of Contents

- Classic Scones with Clotted Cream and Jam
- Earl Grey Shortbread Cookies
- Lemon Drizzle Cake
- Raspberry Almond Tea Cakes
- Earl Grey Infused Madeleines
- Victoria Sponge Cake
- Chocolate-Dipped Biscotti
- Lavender Honey Madeleines
- Cinnamon Sugar Palmiers
- Pistachio and Rose Water Shortbread
- Lemon and Poppy Seed Muffins
- Fruit and Nut Tea Cake
- Mini Lemon Meringue Tarts
- Apricot and Almond Scones
- Ginger and Orange Biscotti
- Carrot and Walnut Tea Loaf
- Cream Cheese and Cucumber Finger Sandwiches
- Strawberry Cream Cheese Danish
- Almond Croissants
- Apple Cinnamon Scones
- Chocolate Hazelnut Tartlets
- Orange Blossom Tea Cakes
- Spiced Chai Cupcakes
- Raspberry and White Chocolate Scones
- Matcha Green Tea Financiers
- Blueberry Lavender Muffins
- Pecan Sandies
- Rose Petal Jam Cookies
- Honey and Lemon Madeleines
- Fig and Walnut Tea Cake
- Mini Victoria Sponge Bites
- Lemon Cream Puffs
- Choco-Mocha Biscotti
- Maple Pecan Tea Loaf
- Almond and Cherry Tarts

- Creamy Earl Grey Truffles
- Hazelnut Espresso Biscuits
- Cardamom Orange Shortbread
- Blackcurrant and Mint Jelly Sandwiches
- Spiced Plum Cake
- Apricot and Almond Danish
- Vanilla Bean Panna Cotta Cups
- Blueberry Lemon Tea Cake
- Almond Raspberry Thumbprint Cookies
- Chocolate Mint Brownies
- Raspberry Lemon Tea Bread
- Cranberry Orange Scones
- Buttermilk Biscuits with Strawberry Jam
- Peach and Cream Cheese Tartlets
- Lemon and Thyme Tea Cookies

Classic Scones with Clotted Cream and Jam

Ingredients:

- 2 cups all-purpose flour
- 1/4 cup sugar
- 1 tbsp baking powder
- 1/2 tsp salt
- 1/2 cup cold unsalted butter, cubed
- 2/3 cup whole milk
- 1 egg (for egg wash)
- Clotted cream and jam (for serving)

Instructions:

1. **Preheat oven**: Preheat your oven to 425°F (220°C). Line a baking sheet with parchment paper.
2. **Prepare dry ingredients**: In a large bowl, sift together flour, sugar, baking powder, and salt.
3. **Cut in butter**: Add cubed cold butter and use a pastry cutter or your fingers to work the butter into the flour until it resembles coarse crumbs.
4. **Add milk**: Gradually add the milk, stirring gently with a spoon until the dough begins to come together. Avoid overworking the dough.
5. **Shape and bake**: Turn the dough onto a floured surface and gently knead it until it's just smooth. Pat the dough to about 1-inch thick and cut into rounds using a cookie cutter. Place on the baking sheet.
6. **Egg wash**: Brush the tops with beaten egg to give them a golden finish.
7. **Bake**: Bake for 10-12 minutes, until golden. Serve warm with clotted cream and jam.

Earl Grey Shortbread Cookies

Ingredients:

- 1 1/2 cups all-purpose flour
- 1/2 cup unsalted butter, softened
- 1/4 cup powdered sugar
- 1 tbsp loose-leaf Earl Grey tea
- 1/4 tsp salt
- 1/2 tsp vanilla extract

Instructions:

1. **Prepare the tea**: Grind the Earl Grey tea leaves into a fine powder using a mortar and pestle or spice grinder.
2. **Mix ingredients**: In a mixing bowl, cream together butter and powdered sugar. Stir in the vanilla extract and salt.
3. **Add flour and tea**: Gradually add the flour and ground tea leaves. Mix until the dough comes together.
4. **Shape the cookies**: Roll the dough into a log or shape into individual cookies. Wrap in plastic wrap and chill in the refrigerator for 30 minutes.
5. **Bake**: Preheat the oven to 325°F (163°C). Slice the dough into rounds and place on a parchment-lined baking sheet. Bake for 10-12 minutes, or until the edges are lightly golden.

Lemon Drizzle Cake

Ingredients:

- 1 cup all-purpose flour
- 1/2 cup butter, softened
- 1/2 cup sugar
- 2 eggs
- 1/2 cup milk
- Zest of 1 lemon
- Juice of 1 lemon
- 1 tsp baking powder
- Pinch of salt
- 1/4 cup powdered sugar (for drizzle)

Instructions:

1. **Preheat oven**: Preheat your oven to 350°F (175°C) and grease a loaf tin.
2. **Make the batter**: In a bowl, cream together butter and sugar until light and fluffy. Beat in eggs, one at a time. Add the lemon zest and juice.
3. **Add dry ingredients**: Sift the flour, baking powder, and salt together. Gradually add to the wet ingredients, alternating with the milk, until smooth.
4. **Bake**: Pour the batter into the loaf tin and bake for 45-50 minutes, or until a skewer comes out clean.
5. **Make the drizzle**: Mix the powdered sugar with lemon juice to create a glaze. Drizzle over the warm cake.

Raspberry Almond Tea Cakes

Ingredients:

- 1 cup all-purpose flour
- 1/2 cup ground almonds
- 1/2 cup sugar
- 1/2 cup unsalted butter, softened
- 2 eggs
- 1/4 tsp almond extract
- 1/4 tsp vanilla extract
- 1/2 cup fresh raspberries

Instructions:

1. **Preheat oven**: Preheat your oven to 350°F (175°C) and grease a muffin tin.
2. **Make the batter**: Cream together butter and sugar. Add eggs one at a time, beating well after each addition. Stir in almond extract and vanilla extract.
3. **Add dry ingredients**: Fold in flour and ground almonds until combined.
4. **Add raspberries**: Gently fold in raspberries.
5. **Bake**: Spoon the batter into the muffin tin and bake for 20-25 minutes, or until golden and a toothpick comes out clean.

Earl Grey Infused Madeleines

Ingredients:

- 1/2 cup unsalted butter, melted
- 1 cup all-purpose flour
- 1/2 cup sugar
- 2 eggs
- 2 tbsp milk
- 1 tbsp Earl Grey tea leaves, finely ground
- 1 tsp vanilla extract
- Pinch of salt
- Powdered sugar (for dusting)

Instructions:

1. **Preheat oven**: Preheat your oven to 375°F (190°C) and grease a Madeleine pan.
2. **Make the batter**: In a bowl, whisk eggs and sugar until pale. Stir in the milk, vanilla extract, and melted butter. Add the ground Earl Grey tea leaves and salt.
3. **Add flour**: Fold in the flour gently until just combined.
4. **Bake**: Spoon the batter into the Madeleine pan and bake for 10-12 minutes, or until lightly golden. Dust with powdered sugar before serving.

Victoria Sponge Cake

Ingredients:

- 1 cup all-purpose flour
- 1 cup sugar
- 1/2 cup unsalted butter, softened
- 2 eggs
- 2 tsp baking powder
- 1/4 cup whole milk
- 1/2 tsp vanilla extract
- Strawberry jam (for filling)
- Whipped cream (for filling)

Instructions:

1. **Preheat oven**: Preheat your oven to 350°F (175°C) and grease two round cake pans.
2. **Make the batter**: Cream together butter and sugar until light and fluffy. Add the eggs one at a time, beating well. Stir in vanilla extract.
3. **Add dry ingredients**: Sift flour and baking powder, then fold into the wet ingredients. Add milk and mix until smooth.
4. **Bake**: Divide the batter between the cake pans and bake for 20-25 minutes, or until a skewer comes out clean.
5. **Assemble**: Once the cakes have cooled, spread a layer of strawberry jam on one layer and top with whipped cream. Sandwich the two layers together.

Chocolate-Dipped Biscotti

Ingredients:

- 1 1/2 cups all-purpose flour
- 1 cup sugar
- 1/2 tsp baking powder
- 1/4 tsp salt
- 1/2 cup unsalted butter, softened
- 2 eggs
- 1 tsp vanilla extract
- 1/2 cup semi-sweet chocolate chips (for dipping)

Instructions:

1. **Preheat oven**: Preheat your oven to 350°F (175°C) and line a baking sheet with parchment paper.
2. **Make the dough**: In a bowl, cream together butter and sugar. Beat in eggs and vanilla. Add flour, baking powder, and salt, mixing until combined.
3. **Shape the dough**: Shape the dough into a log on the baking sheet and flatten slightly.
4. **Bake**: Bake for 25-30 minutes, or until golden. Remove from the oven and let cool for 10 minutes.
5. **Slice and bake again**: Slice the log into biscotti shapes and bake for an additional 10 minutes until crisp.
6. **Dip in chocolate**: Melt the chocolate chips and dip one end of each biscotti into the melted chocolate. Let cool on a wire rack.

Lavender Honey Madeleines

Ingredients:

- 1/2 cup unsalted butter, melted
- 1 cup all-purpose flour
- 1/2 cup sugar
- 2 eggs
- 2 tbsp honey
- 1 tbsp lavender flowers
- 1 tsp vanilla extract
- Pinch of salt
- Powdered sugar (for dusting)

Instructions:

1. **Preheat oven**: Preheat your oven to 375°F (190°C) and grease a Madeleine pan.
2. **Infuse the butter**: Melt the butter in a saucepan and add the lavender flowers. Let it infuse for 5 minutes and strain it.
3. **Make the batter**: In a bowl, whisk eggs and sugar until pale. Stir in honey, vanilla extract, and the infused butter.
4. **Add dry ingredients**: Fold in the flour and salt until just combined.
5. **Bake**: Spoon the batter into the Madeleine pan and bake for 10-12 minutes, or until lightly golden. Dust with powdered sugar before serving.

Cinnamon Sugar Palmiers

Ingredients:

- 1 sheet puff pastry, thawed
- 1/4 cup granulated sugar
- 1 tsp ground cinnamon
- 1/4 cup butter, melted

Instructions:

1. **Preheat oven**: Preheat your oven to 400°F (200°C) and line a baking sheet with parchment paper.
2. **Prepare the pastry**: Roll out the puff pastry sheet on a lightly floured surface. Brush with melted butter.
3. **Make cinnamon sugar**: Mix the granulated sugar and cinnamon in a small bowl.
4. **Add the filling**: Sprinkle the cinnamon sugar evenly over the buttered pastry.
5. **Shape the palmiers**: Fold the two opposite edges of the pastry toward the center so they meet in the middle. Fold again to create a long log. Slice the log into 1-inch pieces.
6. **Bake**: Place the slices on the baking sheet, spacing them apart. Bake for 10-12 minutes, or until golden and puffed.

Pistachio and Rose Water Shortbread

Ingredients:

- 1 cup all-purpose flour
- 1/2 cup unsalted butter, softened
- 1/4 cup powdered sugar
- 1/4 cup pistachios, finely chopped
- 1 tsp rose water
- 1/4 tsp salt

Instructions:

1. **Preheat oven**: Preheat your oven to 325°F (163°C) and line a baking sheet with parchment paper.
2. **Make the dough**: In a bowl, cream together the butter and powdered sugar until light and fluffy. Stir in the rose water and salt.
3. **Add dry ingredients**: Gradually add the flour, mixing until the dough forms. Fold in the chopped pistachios.
4. **Shape the cookies**: Roll out the dough on a lightly floured surface and cut into shapes using a cookie cutter or slice into rectangles.
5. **Bake**: Place the cookies on the prepared baking sheet and bake for 10-12 minutes or until the edges are lightly golden.

Lemon and Poppy Seed Muffins

Ingredients:

- 1 1/2 cups all-purpose flour
- 1/2 cup sugar
- 2 tsp baking powder
- 1/4 tsp salt
- 1/4 cup poppy seeds
- 1/2 cup whole milk
- 1/4 cup unsalted butter, melted
- 2 eggs
- Zest of 1 lemon
- Juice of 1 lemon

Instructions:

1. **Preheat oven**: Preheat your oven to 375°F (190°C) and grease a muffin tin.
2. **Mix dry ingredients**: In a bowl, combine flour, sugar, baking powder, salt, and poppy seeds.
3. **Mix wet ingredients**: In another bowl, whisk together milk, butter, eggs, lemon zest, and lemon juice.
4. **Combine**: Gradually add the wet ingredients to the dry ingredients and stir until just combined.
5. **Bake**: Spoon the batter into the muffin tin and bake for 18-20 minutes, or until a toothpick comes out clean.

Fruit and Nut Tea Cake

Ingredients:

- 1 1/2 cups mixed dried fruit (raisins, currants, sultanas)
- 1/2 cup chopped nuts (walnuts, almonds)
- 1/2 cup unsalted butter, softened
- 1/2 cup brown sugar
- 2 eggs
- 1 1/2 cups all-purpose flour
- 1 tsp baking powder
- 1/4 tsp salt
- 1/2 tsp cinnamon
- 1/4 tsp ground nutmeg
- 1/2 cup milk

Instructions:

1. **Preheat oven**: Preheat your oven to 325°F (163°C) and grease a loaf tin.
2. **Prepare the fruit**: In a small bowl, combine the dried fruit with a tablespoon of flour to coat. Set aside.
3. **Make the batter**: Cream together butter and brown sugar until light. Add eggs one at a time, beating well after each addition.
4. **Add dry ingredients**: In a separate bowl, mix flour, baking powder, salt, cinnamon, and nutmeg. Gradually fold this into the wet ingredients, alternating with the milk.
5. **Add fruit and nuts**: Fold in the flour-coated dried fruit and nuts.
6. **Bake**: Pour the batter into the loaf tin and bake for 50-60 minutes, or until a toothpick inserted comes out clean.

Mini Lemon Meringue Tarts

Ingredients:

- 1 package tartlet shells (store-bought or homemade)
- 1/2 cup sugar
- 3 tbsp cornstarch
- 1 1/2 cups water
- 3 egg yolks
- 1/4 cup lemon juice
- 1 tbsp lemon zest
- 1/4 tsp salt
- 3 egg whites
- 1/4 tsp cream of tartar

Instructions:

1. **Make the lemon filling**: In a saucepan, combine sugar, cornstarch, water, and salt. Bring to a boil, whisking constantly until thickened.
2. **Temper the eggs**: In a separate bowl, whisk the egg yolks. Gradually add a little of the hot mixture to the yolks to temper them, then slowly add the yolks back into the saucepan. Stir in lemon juice and zest. Cook for an additional 2-3 minutes until smooth.
3. **Make the meringue**: Whip egg whites with cream of tartar until stiff peaks form. Gradually add sugar and continue beating until glossy.
4. **Assemble the tarts**: Spoon the lemon filling into the tartlet shells. Top with a dollop of meringue and use a spoon to create swirls.
5. **Bake**: Preheat the oven to 350°F (175°C) and bake the tarts for 10-12 minutes or until the meringue is golden.

Apricot and Almond Scones

Ingredients:

- 2 cups all-purpose flour
- 1/4 cup sugar
- 1 tbsp baking powder
- 1/2 tsp salt
- 1/2 cup unsalted butter, cold and cubed
- 1/2 cup dried apricots, chopped
- 1/4 cup slivered almonds
- 1/2 cup buttermilk

Instructions:

1. **Preheat oven**: Preheat your oven to 375°F (190°C) and line a baking sheet with parchment paper.
2. **Prepare the dry ingredients**: In a large bowl, whisk together flour, sugar, baking powder, and salt.
3. **Cut in the butter**: Add the cubed butter and use a pastry cutter or your fingers to work it into the flour mixture until it resembles coarse crumbs.
4. **Add fruit and nuts**: Stir in the chopped apricots and slivered almonds.
5. **Add buttermilk**: Pour in the buttermilk and stir gently until the dough just comes together.
6. **Shape and bake**: Turn the dough onto a floured surface, pat it into a circle, and cut it into wedges. Place the wedges on the baking sheet and bake for 15-20 minutes, or until golden brown.

Ginger and Orange Biscotti

Ingredients:

- 1 1/2 cups all-purpose flour
- 1/2 cup sugar
- 1/2 tsp baking powder
- 1/4 tsp salt
- 1/2 tsp ground ginger
- 1/2 tsp orange zest
- 1/4 cup unsalted butter, softened
- 2 eggs
- 1/4 cup crystallized ginger, chopped
- 1/4 cup chopped almonds

Instructions:

1. **Preheat oven**: Preheat your oven to 350°F (175°C) and line a baking sheet with parchment paper.
2. **Make the dough**: In a bowl, whisk together flour, sugar, baking powder, salt, ginger, and orange zest. Add the butter and mix until combined. Stir in eggs one at a time until smooth.
3. **Add mix-ins**: Fold in crystallized ginger and chopped almonds.
4. **Shape the dough**: Shape the dough into a log and place it on the baking sheet.
5. **Bake**: Bake for 20-25 minutes, then remove and let cool slightly before slicing into biscotti shapes. Bake the slices again for 10-12 minutes to crisp them up.

Carrot and Walnut Tea Loaf

Ingredients:

- 1 1/2 cups all-purpose flour
- 1/2 cup brown sugar
- 1 tsp baking powder
- 1/2 tsp baking soda
- 1/4 tsp salt
- 1/2 tsp ground cinnamon
- 2 eggs
- 1/2 cup vegetable oil
- 1 tsp vanilla extract
- 1 cup grated carrots
- 1/2 cup chopped walnuts

Instructions:

1. **Preheat oven**: Preheat your oven to 350°F (175°C) and grease a loaf tin.
2. **Mix dry ingredients**: In a bowl, combine flour, sugar, baking powder, baking soda, salt, and cinnamon.
3. **Make the batter**: In another bowl, whisk together eggs, oil, and vanilla. Gradually add the dry ingredients and mix until just combined. Fold in the grated carrots and walnuts.
4. **Bake**: Pour the batter into the loaf tin and bake for 45-50 minutes, or until a toothpick comes out clean.

Cream Cheese and Cucumber Finger Sandwiches

Ingredients:

- 8 slices white or whole grain bread
- 4 oz cream cheese, softened
- 1 tbsp fresh dill, chopped
- 1 tbsp lemon juice
- 1 cucumber, thinly sliced
- Salt and pepper to taste

Instructions:

1. **Prepare the spread**: In a small bowl, mix the cream cheese, dill, and lemon juice until smooth. Season with salt and pepper.
2. **Assemble the sandwiches**: Spread the cream cheese mixture evenly on one side of each slice of bread.
3. **Add the cucumber**: Layer the thin cucumber slices on top of the cream cheese.
4. **Trim and serve**: Trim the crusts off the bread and cut the sandwiches into finger-sized pieces. Serve immediately or refrigerate until ready to serve.

Strawberry Cream Cheese Danish

Ingredients:

- 1 sheet puff pastry, thawed
- 4 oz cream cheese, softened
- 1/4 cup powdered sugar
- 1 tsp vanilla extract
- 1/2 cup fresh strawberries, diced
- 1 tbsp sugar
- 1 egg (for egg wash)

Instructions:

1. **Preheat oven**: Preheat your oven to 375°F (190°C) and line a baking sheet with parchment paper.
2. **Prepare the filling**: In a bowl, mix the cream cheese, powdered sugar, and vanilla extract until smooth.
3. **Assemble the danish**: Roll out the puff pastry and cut it into squares. Spread a spoonful of the cream cheese mixture in the center of each square. Top with diced strawberries and sprinkle with a little sugar.
4. **Shape the danish**: Fold the corners of each square toward the center to form a pocket, leaving the center exposed.
5. **Egg wash**: Brush the edges with the egg wash (beaten egg).
6. **Bake**: Bake for 15-20 minutes or until the pastry is golden and puffed. Let cool before serving.

Almond Croissants

Ingredients:

- 4 croissants, halved
- 1/2 cup almond paste
- 1/4 cup powdered sugar
- 2 tbsp unsalted butter, softened
- 1/4 tsp almond extract
- 1 egg (for egg wash)
- Sliced almonds for topping

Instructions:

1. **Preheat oven**: Preheat your oven to 375°F (190°C) and line a baking sheet with parchment paper.
2. **Make the almond filling**: In a bowl, combine the almond paste, powdered sugar, butter, and almond extract until smooth.
3. **Fill the croissants**: Spread a generous amount of the almond filling inside the halved croissants.
4. **Egg wash**: Brush the top of the croissants with a beaten egg.
5. **Bake**: Place the croissants on the baking sheet and sprinkle with sliced almonds. Bake for 15-20 minutes or until golden and crispy.

Apple Cinnamon Scones

Ingredients:

- 2 cups all-purpose flour
- 1/4 cup sugar
- 1 tbsp baking powder
- 1/4 tsp salt
- 1 tsp ground cinnamon
- 1/2 cup unsalted butter, cold and cubed
- 1 apple, peeled and finely chopped
- 1/2 cup heavy cream
- 1 egg
- 1 tbsp milk (for brushing)

Instructions:

1. **Preheat oven**: Preheat your oven to 375°F (190°C) and line a baking sheet with parchment paper.
2. **Mix dry ingredients**: In a bowl, whisk together flour, sugar, baking powder, salt, and cinnamon.
3. **Cut in the butter**: Add the cold butter and cut it into the flour mixture using a pastry cutter or your fingers until it resembles coarse crumbs.
4. **Add apples and cream**: Stir in the chopped apples. In a separate bowl, whisk together the cream and egg, then add to the dry mixture. Mix until just combined.
5. **Shape and bake**: Turn the dough onto a floured surface, pat it into a circle, and cut into wedges. Place the wedges on the baking sheet and brush with milk. Bake for 20-25 minutes until golden.

Chocolate Hazelnut Tartlets

Ingredients:

- 1 package tartlet shells (store-bought or homemade)
- 1/2 cup hazelnut spread (like Nutella)
- 4 oz dark chocolate, chopped
- 1/4 cup heavy cream
- 1/4 cup chopped toasted hazelnuts

Instructions:

1. **Prepare the tartlets**: Pre-bake the tartlet shells according to package instructions if using store-bought, or prepare them from scratch.
2. **Make the chocolate ganache**: Heat the heavy cream in a saucepan until just simmering. Remove from heat and add the chopped chocolate, stirring until smooth.
3. **Assemble the tartlets**: Spread a thin layer of hazelnut spread inside each tartlet shell. Pour the chocolate ganache over the hazelnut spread and smooth it out.
4. **Top with hazelnuts**: Sprinkle the chopped toasted hazelnuts on top.
5. **Chill**: Allow the tartlets to set in the refrigerator for at least an hour before serving.

Orange Blossom Tea Cakes

Ingredients:

- 1 1/2 cups all-purpose flour
- 1/2 cup butter, softened
- 1/4 cup sugar
- 1 egg
- 1 tbsp orange blossom water
- 1/4 tsp salt
- 1/2 tsp baking powder
- Zest of 1 orange

Instructions:

1. **Preheat oven**: Preheat your oven to 350°F (175°C) and grease a baking sheet.
2. **Make the dough**: In a bowl, cream the butter and sugar together until light and fluffy. Add the egg, orange blossom water, orange zest, and mix until smooth.
3. **Add dry ingredients**: In a separate bowl, whisk together flour, salt, and baking powder. Gradually add the dry ingredients to the wet mixture and mix until combined.
4. **Shape the cakes**: Drop spoonfuls of dough onto the prepared baking sheet. Flatten slightly with the back of a spoon.
5. **Bake**: Bake for 12-15 minutes or until lightly golden. Let cool on a wire rack.

Spiced Chai Cupcakes

Ingredients:

- 1 1/2 cups all-purpose flour
- 1 tsp ground cinnamon
- 1/2 tsp ground ginger
- 1/4 tsp ground cloves
- 1/4 tsp ground cardamom
- 1/2 tsp baking powder
- 1/4 tsp baking soda
- 1/4 tsp salt
- 1/2 cup unsalted butter, softened
- 1 cup sugar
- 2 eggs
- 1 tsp vanilla extract
- 1/2 cup milk
- 1/2 cup strong chai tea (cooled)

Instructions:

1. **Preheat oven**: Preheat your oven to 350°F (175°C) and line a muffin tin with paper liners.
2. **Mix dry ingredients**: In a bowl, whisk together flour, cinnamon, ginger, cloves, cardamom, baking powder, baking soda, and salt.
3. **Cream the butter and sugar**: In a separate bowl, cream together butter and sugar until light and fluffy. Add eggs one at a time, beating well after each addition. Stir in vanilla extract.
4. **Add milk and tea**: Gradually add the dry ingredients, alternating with milk and chai tea. Mix until just combined.
5. **Bake**: Fill the muffin tin with batter and bake for 18-20 minutes or until a toothpick comes out clean.

Raspberry and White Chocolate Scones

Ingredients:

- 2 cups all-purpose flour
- 1/4 cup sugar
- 1 tbsp baking powder
- 1/4 tsp salt
- 1/2 cup unsalted butter, cold and cubed
- 1/2 cup raspberries
- 1/4 cup white chocolate chips
- 1/2 cup buttermilk
- 1 egg (for egg wash)

Instructions:

1. **Preheat oven**: Preheat your oven to 375°F (190°C) and line a baking sheet with parchment paper.
2. **Mix dry ingredients**: In a bowl, whisk together flour, sugar, baking powder, and salt.
3. **Cut in the butter**: Add the cold butter and work it into the dry ingredients until the mixture resembles coarse crumbs.
4. **Add the berries and chocolate**: Gently fold in the raspberries and white chocolate chips.
5. **Shape the scones**: Add the buttermilk and mix gently until the dough just comes together. Turn the dough out onto a floured surface, shape into a circle, and cut into wedges.
6. **Egg wash**: Brush the tops with a beaten egg.
7. **Bake**: Place the scones on the baking sheet and bake for 18-20 minutes, or until golden brown.

Matcha Green Tea Financiers

Ingredients:

- 1/2 cup almond flour
- 1/2 cup all-purpose flour
- 1/4 cup powdered sugar
- 2 tbsp matcha powder
- 1/2 tsp baking powder
- 1/4 tsp salt
- 4 oz unsalted butter, melted
- 4 egg whites
- 1 tsp vanilla extract

Instructions:

1. **Preheat oven**: Preheat your oven to 375°F (190°C) and grease a financier mold or mini muffin tin.
2. **Dry ingredients**: In a bowl, whisk together almond flour, all-purpose flour, powdered sugar, matcha powder, baking powder, and salt.
3. **Wet ingredients**: In a separate bowl, whisk egg whites until frothy but not stiff. Add the melted butter and vanilla extract to the egg whites.
4. **Combine**: Gently fold the wet ingredients into the dry ingredients until fully combined.
5. **Bake**: Pour the batter into the molds and bake for 12-15 minutes, or until golden and a toothpick inserted comes out clean. Let cool before removing from the mold.

Blueberry Lavender Muffins

Ingredients:

- 2 cups all-purpose flour
- 1 cup sugar
- 2 tsp baking powder
- 1/2 tsp baking soda
- 1/4 tsp salt
- 1/2 tsp dried lavender buds
- 1/2 cup milk
- 1/2 cup unsalted butter, melted
- 1 egg
- 1 tsp vanilla extract
- 1 1/2 cups fresh blueberries

Instructions:

1. **Preheat oven**: Preheat your oven to 350°F (175°C) and line a muffin tin with paper liners.
2. **Mix dry ingredients**: In a large bowl, whisk together flour, sugar, baking powder, baking soda, salt, and lavender.
3. **Mix wet ingredients**: In a separate bowl, whisk together milk, melted butter, egg, and vanilla extract.
4. **Combine**: Pour the wet ingredients into the dry ingredients and stir until just combined. Gently fold in the blueberries.
5. **Bake**: Spoon the batter into the muffin tin and bake for 18-20 minutes or until a toothpick comes out clean.

Pecan Sandies

Ingredients:

- 1 cup unsalted butter, softened
- 1/2 cup powdered sugar
- 2 cups all-purpose flour
- 1/2 tsp salt
- 1 cup pecans, chopped
- 1/2 tsp vanilla extract

Instructions:

1. **Preheat oven**: Preheat your oven to 350°F (175°C) and line a baking sheet with parchment paper.
2. **Cream butter and sugar**: In a bowl, cream together butter and powdered sugar until smooth.
3. **Add flour and salt**: Gradually add flour and salt to the butter mixture, mixing until fully incorporated.
4. **Add pecans**: Stir in the chopped pecans and vanilla extract.
5. **Shape cookies**: Roll the dough into small balls and flatten with a fork. Place them on the baking sheet.
6. **Bake**: Bake for 12-15 minutes, or until the edges are lightly golden. Let cool before serving.

Rose Petal Jam Cookies

Ingredients:

- 1 cup unsalted butter, softened
- 3/4 cup sugar
- 2 cups all-purpose flour
- 1/4 tsp salt
- 1/4 cup rose petal jam (or other floral jam)
- 1 tsp vanilla extract
- Powdered sugar for dusting

Instructions:

1. **Preheat oven**: Preheat your oven to 350°F (175°C) and line a baking sheet with parchment paper.
2. **Cream butter and sugar**: In a bowl, cream together butter and sugar until light and fluffy.
3. **Add dry ingredients**: Gradually mix in the flour and salt.
4. **Assemble cookies**: Scoop out a spoonful of dough, roll it into a ball, and flatten slightly on the baking sheet. Make a small indentation in the center of each cookie and add a small spoonful of rose petal jam.
5. **Bake**: Bake for 12-15 minutes, or until golden. Allow the cookies to cool before dusting with powdered sugar.

Honey and Lemon Madeleines

Ingredients:

- 1/2 cup unsalted butter, melted
- 1 cup all-purpose flour
- 1/2 tsp baking powder
- 1/4 tsp salt
- 1/2 cup sugar
- 2 large eggs
- 1 tbsp honey
- Zest of 1 lemon
- 1 tbsp fresh lemon juice

Instructions:

1. **Preheat oven**: Preheat your oven to 350°F (175°C) and grease a madeleine pan.
2. **Dry ingredients**: In a bowl, whisk together flour, baking powder, and salt.
3. **Wet ingredients**: In a separate bowl, whisk eggs and sugar until light and fluffy. Stir in honey, lemon zest, and lemon juice.
4. **Combine**: Gradually add the dry ingredients to the wet ingredients and mix until smooth. Stir in the melted butter.
5. **Bake**: Spoon the batter into the madeleine pan and bake for 10-12 minutes, or until golden brown. Let cool before serving.

Fig and Walnut Tea Cake

Ingredients:

- 1 cup all-purpose flour
- 1 tsp baking powder
- 1/4 tsp salt
- 1/2 cup unsalted butter, softened
- 1/2 cup brown sugar
- 2 large eggs
- 1/2 cup milk
- 1/2 tsp vanilla extract
- 1 cup dried figs, chopped
- 1/2 cup walnuts, chopped

Instructions:

1. **Preheat oven**: Preheat your oven to 350°F (175°C) and grease a loaf pan.
2. **Mix dry ingredients**: In a bowl, whisk together flour, baking powder, and salt.
3. **Cream butter and sugar**: In a separate bowl, cream together butter and brown sugar until light and fluffy. Add the eggs, one at a time, beating well after each addition.
4. **Add wet ingredients**: Stir in milk and vanilla extract.
5. **Combine**: Gradually add the dry ingredients and mix until just combined. Fold in the chopped figs and walnuts.
6. **Bake**: Pour the batter into the loaf pan and bake for 40-45 minutes, or until a toothpick comes out clean. Let cool before slicing.

Mini Victoria Sponge Bites

Ingredients:

- 1 cup all-purpose flour
- 1/2 cup sugar
- 1 tsp baking powder
- 1/2 cup unsalted butter, softened
- 2 large eggs
- 1 tsp vanilla extract
- 1/4 cup strawberry jam
- Powdered sugar for dusting

Instructions:

1. **Preheat oven**: Preheat your oven to 350°F (175°C) and grease a mini muffin tin.
2. **Mix dry ingredients**: In a bowl, whisk together flour, sugar, and baking powder.
3. **Cream butter and sugar**: In another bowl, cream together butter and sugar until light and fluffy. Add eggs one at a time, followed by vanilla extract.
4. **Combine**: Gradually mix in the dry ingredients until smooth.
5. **Bake**: Spoon the batter into the muffin tin and bake for 12-15 minutes, or until golden and a toothpick comes out clean.
6. **Assemble**: Once the mini cakes have cooled, slice them in half and spread strawberry jam in the middle. Dust with powdered sugar before serving.

Lemon Cream Puffs

Ingredients:

- 1/2 cup water
- 1/2 cup unsalted butter
- 1 cup all-purpose flour
- 1/4 tsp salt
- 4 large eggs
- 1/2 cup heavy cream
- 2 tbsp powdered sugar
- 1 tbsp lemon zest
- 1 tbsp fresh lemon juice

Instructions:

1. **Preheat oven**: Preheat your oven to 375°F (190°C) and line a baking sheet with parchment paper.
2. **Make the choux pastry**: In a saucepan, bring water and butter to a boil. Remove from heat and stir in flour and salt until smooth. Let cool slightly. Add the eggs, one at a time, mixing well after each addition.
3. **Pipe the dough**: Using a piping bag, pipe small rounds of dough onto the baking sheet.
4. **Bake**: Bake for 20-25 minutes, or until golden and puffed. Let cool.
5. **Make the filling**: Whisk together heavy cream, powdered sugar, lemon zest, and lemon juice until stiff peaks form.
6. **Assemble**: Slice the cream puffs in half and fill with the lemon cream. Serve immediately.

Choco-Mocha Biscotti

Ingredients:

- 1 1/2 cups all-purpose flour
- 1/2 cup cocoa powder
- 1 tsp baking powder
- 1/2 tsp salt
- 1/2 cup unsalted butter, softened
- 3/4 cup sugar
- 2 large eggs
- 1 tbsp instant coffee granules
- 1 tsp vanilla extract
- 1 cup semi-sweet chocolate chips
- 1/2 cup chopped walnuts (optional)

Instructions:

1. **Preheat oven**: Preheat your oven to 350°F (175°C) and line a baking sheet with parchment paper.
2. **Combine dry ingredients**: In a bowl, whisk together flour, cocoa powder, baking powder, and salt.
3. **Cream butter and sugar**: In a large bowl, cream together butter and sugar until light and fluffy. Add the eggs, one at a time, beating well after each addition.
4. **Add coffee and vanilla**: Dissolve the coffee granules in a tablespoon of warm water and add to the butter mixture along with vanilla extract.
5. **Add dry ingredients**: Gradually fold in the dry ingredients and mix until combined. Stir in chocolate chips and walnuts if using.
6. **Shape and bake**: Divide the dough into two logs and place them on the baking sheet. Bake for 25 minutes, or until firm and slightly cracked. Let cool for 10 minutes, then slice into 1/2-inch wide pieces.
7. **Bake again**: Lay the slices flat on the baking sheet and bake for an additional 10-12 minutes until crisp. Let cool completely.

Maple Pecan Tea Loaf

Ingredients:

- 1 cup all-purpose flour
- 1 tsp baking powder
- 1/2 tsp salt
- 1/2 cup unsalted butter, softened
- 1/2 cup brown sugar
- 2 large eggs
- 1/2 cup maple syrup
- 1/2 cup chopped pecans
- 1 tsp vanilla extract
- 1/2 cup milk

Instructions:

1. **Preheat oven**: Preheat your oven to 350°F (175°C) and grease a loaf pan.
2. **Mix dry ingredients**: In a bowl, whisk together flour, baking powder, and salt.
3. **Cream butter and sugar**: In another bowl, cream together butter and brown sugar until light and fluffy. Add the eggs, one at a time, beating well after each addition.
4. **Add wet ingredients**: Stir in maple syrup, vanilla extract, and milk until combined.
5. **Combine**: Gradually add the dry ingredients and mix until just combined. Fold in chopped pecans.
6. **Bake**: Pour the batter into the prepared loaf pan and bake for 50-60 minutes or until a toothpick inserted comes out clean. Let cool before serving.

Almond and Cherry Tarts

Ingredients:

- 1 1/4 cups all-purpose flour
- 1/4 cup powdered sugar
- 1/2 cup unsalted butter, cold and cubed
- 1 egg yolk
- 1/4 tsp almond extract
- 1/4 cup almond meal
- 1/2 cup cherry preserves
- Sliced almonds for topping

Instructions:

1. **Preheat oven**: Preheat your oven to 375°F (190°C) and grease a tartlet pan.
2. **Make the crust**: In a food processor, pulse flour, powdered sugar, and cold butter until the mixture resembles coarse crumbs. Add egg yolk and almond extract, and pulse until the dough comes together.
3. **Chill the dough**: Roll the dough into a ball, wrap in plastic, and chill for at least 30 minutes.
4. **Form the tartlets**: Roll out the dough on a floured surface and cut into circles to fit into the tartlet pan. Press the dough into the pan and fill each tart with a spoonful of cherry preserves.
5. **Bake**: Top each tart with a sprinkle of almond meal and sliced almonds. Bake for 15-20 minutes until golden. Allow to cool before serving.

Creamy Earl Grey Truffles

Ingredients:

- 8 oz dark chocolate, chopped
- 1/2 cup heavy cream
- 2 tbsp Earl Grey tea leaves
- 1 tbsp unsalted butter
- Cocoa powder for coating

Instructions:

1. **Infuse cream**: Heat heavy cream in a small saucepan over medium heat. Add the Earl Grey tea leaves and bring to a simmer. Remove from heat and let steep for 5-10 minutes. Strain the cream to remove the tea leaves.
2. **Make the ganache**: Pour the infused cream over the chopped dark chocolate and let sit for 2-3 minutes. Stir until smooth and creamy. Add butter and stir until melted.
3. **Chill the mixture**: Allow the ganache to cool to room temperature, then refrigerate for 1-2 hours until firm.
4. **Form truffles**: Once the ganache is firm, scoop small portions and roll them into balls. Coat the truffles in cocoa powder. Store in the fridge until ready to serve.

Hazelnut Espresso Biscuits

Ingredients:

- 1 1/2 cups all-purpose flour
- 1/4 cup ground espresso coffee
- 1/2 cup hazelnuts, chopped
- 1/2 tsp baking powder
- 1/4 tsp salt
- 1/2 cup unsalted butter, softened
- 1/2 cup sugar
- 1 large egg
- 1 tsp vanilla extract

Instructions:

1. **Preheat oven**: Preheat your oven to 350°F (175°C) and line a baking sheet with parchment paper.
2. **Combine dry ingredients**: In a bowl, whisk together flour, ground espresso coffee, baking powder, and salt.
3. **Cream butter and sugar**: In a separate bowl, cream together butter and sugar until light and fluffy. Add the egg and vanilla extract, and mix until combined.
4. **Combine**: Gradually add the dry ingredients to the wet ingredients and mix until just combined. Stir in chopped hazelnuts.
5. **Shape biscuits**: Roll the dough into small balls and flatten slightly on the baking sheet.
6. **Bake**: Bake for 12-15 minutes, or until the biscuits are golden. Let cool before serving.

Cardamom Orange Shortbread

Ingredients:

- 1 1/2 cups all-purpose flour
- 1/2 cup cornstarch
- 1/2 tsp ground cardamom
- Zest of 1 orange
- 1/2 cup unsalted butter, softened
- 1/4 cup powdered sugar
- 1/4 cup granulated sugar

Instructions:

1. **Preheat oven**: Preheat your oven to 350°F (175°C) and line a baking sheet with parchment paper.
2. **Mix dry ingredients**: In a bowl, whisk together flour, cornstarch, cardamom, and orange zest.
3. **Cream butter and sugars**: In a separate bowl, cream together butter, powdered sugar, and granulated sugar until light and fluffy.
4. **Combine**: Gradually add the dry ingredients and mix until a soft dough forms.
5. **Shape cookies**: Roll the dough into small balls, flatten slightly, and place on the baking sheet.
6. **Bake**: Bake for 12-15 minutes, or until the edges are lightly golden. Let cool before serving.

Blackcurrant and Mint Jelly Sandwiches

Ingredients:

- 1 loaf of white or whole wheat bread, crusts removed
- 1/2 cup blackcurrant jelly
- Fresh mint leaves, chopped
- Butter (optional)

Instructions:

1. **Prepare bread**: Spread butter on the bread slices, if desired. Spread a thin layer of blackcurrant jelly on one slice of each sandwich.
2. **Add mint**: Sprinkle the chopped mint leaves over the jelly.
3. **Assemble**: Place the other slice of bread on top and press gently.
4. **Cut and serve**: Cut into small finger sandwiches and serve.

Spiced Plum Cake

Ingredients:

- 2 cups all-purpose flour
- 1 tsp baking powder
- 1/2 tsp ground cinnamon
- 1/4 tsp ground cloves
- 1/4 tsp ground nutmeg
- 1/4 tsp ground ginger
- 1/2 cup unsalted butter, softened
- 1 cup brown sugar
- 2 large eggs
- 1/2 cup buttermilk
- 2 cups plums, pitted and chopped
- 1/2 cup chopped walnuts (optional)

Instructions:

1. **Preheat oven**: Preheat your oven to 350°F (175°C) and grease a loaf pan.
2. **Mix dry ingredients**: In a bowl, whisk together flour, baking powder, and spices.
3. **Cream butter and sugar**: In a separate bowl, cream together butter and sugar until light and fluffy. Add eggs one at a time, mixing well after each addition.
4. **Add wet ingredients**: Stir in the buttermilk.
5. **Combine**: Gradually add the dry ingredients to the wet ingredients and mix until just combined. Fold in the plums and walnuts.
6. **Bake**: Pour the batter into the prepared loaf pan and bake for 55-60 minutes, or until a toothpick comes out clean. Let cool before serving.

Apricot and Almond Danish

Ingredients:

- 1 package puff pastry (store-bought or homemade)
- 1/2 cup apricot preserves
- 1/4 cup almond meal
- 1/4 cup sugar
- 1/2 tsp almond extract
- 1/4 cup sliced almonds
- 1 egg (for egg wash)

Instructions:

1. **Preheat oven**: Preheat your oven to 375°F (190°C) and line a baking sheet with parchment paper.
2. **Prepare the pastry**: Roll out the puff pastry on a lightly floured surface. Cut into squares (about 4x4 inches).
3. **Make filling**: In a small bowl, mix almond meal, sugar, and almond extract.
4. **Assemble the Danish**: Place a spoonful of almond mixture in the center of each pastry square. Top with a spoonful of apricot preserves and a few sliced almonds.
5. **Fold and brush**: Fold the corners of the pastry squares to form a pocket. Beat the egg and brush over the pastry edges for a golden finish.
6. **Bake**: Place on the baking sheet and bake for 20-25 minutes, or until golden and puffed. Allow to cool before serving.

Vanilla Bean Panna Cotta Cups

Ingredients:

- 2 cups heavy cream
- 1 cup whole milk
- 1/2 cup sugar
- 1 vanilla bean (split and scraped) or 2 tsp vanilla extract
- 2 1/4 tsp gelatin
- 1/4 cup cold water

Instructions:

1. **Bloom the gelatin**: In a small bowl, sprinkle gelatin over cold water and let it sit for 5-10 minutes to bloom.
2. **Heat the cream**: In a saucepan, combine heavy cream, milk, and sugar. Heat over medium heat until sugar is dissolved and the cream is just about to simmer.
3. **Add vanilla**: Add the vanilla bean seeds or vanilla extract to the cream mixture.
4. **Dissolve the gelatin**: Stir the bloomed gelatin into the warm cream mixture until fully dissolved. Remove from heat.
5. **Chill**: Pour the mixture into small cups or molds and refrigerate for at least 4 hours or until set.
6. **Serve**: Serve chilled, optionally topped with fresh berries or fruit compote.

Blueberry Lemon Tea Cake

Ingredients:

- 1 1/2 cups all-purpose flour
- 1 tsp baking powder
- 1/2 tsp baking soda
- 1/4 tsp salt
- 1/2 cup unsalted butter, softened
- 1 cup sugar
- 2 large eggs
- 1 tsp vanilla extract
- Zest and juice of 1 lemon
- 1/2 cup sour cream
- 1 cup fresh or frozen blueberries
- Powdered sugar (for dusting)

Instructions:

1. **Preheat oven**: Preheat your oven to 350°F (175°C) and grease a loaf pan.
2. **Mix dry ingredients**: In a bowl, whisk together flour, baking powder, baking soda, and salt.
3. **Cream butter and sugar**: In a separate bowl, beat together butter and sugar until light and fluffy. Add the eggs one at a time, beating well after each addition.
4. **Add flavorings**: Stir in vanilla extract, lemon zest, and lemon juice. Add the sour cream and mix until smooth.
5. **Combine**: Gradually add the dry ingredients and mix until just combined. Gently fold in the blueberries.
6. **Bake**: Pour the batter into the prepared loaf pan and bake for 50-60 minutes or until a toothpick comes out clean. Let cool and dust with powdered sugar before serving.

Almond Raspberry Thumbprint Cookies

Ingredients:

- 1 cup unsalted butter, softened
- 1/2 cup powdered sugar
- 1 tsp vanilla extract
- 1/2 tsp almond extract
- 2 cups all-purpose flour
- 1/4 tsp salt
- 1/2 cup raspberry jam
- 1/4 cup sliced almonds

Instructions:

1. **Preheat oven**: Preheat your oven to 350°F (175°C) and line a baking sheet with parchment paper.
2. **Cream butter and sugar**: Beat together butter and powdered sugar until creamy and light. Add vanilla and almond extracts, and mix.
3. **Add dry ingredients**: Gradually add flour and salt, mixing until the dough comes together.
4. **Form cookies**: Roll dough into 1-inch balls and place on the baking sheet. Use your thumb to create an indentation in the center of each cookie.
5. **Fill and top**: Spoon a small amount of raspberry jam into each indentation and top with sliced almonds.
6. **Bake**: Bake for 12-15 minutes, or until the edges are lightly golden. Let cool before serving.

Chocolate Mint Brownies

Ingredients:

- 1/2 cup unsalted butter, melted
- 1 cup sugar
- 2 large eggs
- 1 tsp vanilla extract
- 1/3 cup unsweetened cocoa powder
- 1/2 cup all-purpose flour
- 1/4 tsp salt
- 1/4 tsp baking powder
- 1/2 cup mint chocolate chips
- 1/2 cup dark chocolate chips

Instructions:

1. **Preheat oven**: Preheat your oven to 350°F (175°C) and grease a baking pan.
2. **Make batter**: In a large bowl, whisk together melted butter and sugar. Add eggs and vanilla extract, and mix well. Stir in cocoa powder, flour, salt, and baking powder until smooth.
3. **Add chocolate chips**: Fold in mint chocolate chips and dark chocolate chips.
4. **Bake**: Pour the batter into the prepared pan and bake for 20-25 minutes, or until a toothpick inserted comes out with a few moist crumbs.
5. **Cool and serve**: Let cool completely in the pan before cutting into squares and serving.

Raspberry Lemon Tea Bread

Ingredients:

- 1 1/2 cups all-purpose flour
- 1 tsp baking powder
- 1/2 tsp baking soda
- 1/4 tsp salt
- 1/2 cup unsalted butter, softened
- 1 cup sugar
- 2 large eggs
- Zest and juice of 1 lemon
- 1 tsp vanilla extract
- 1/2 cup buttermilk
- 1 cup fresh raspberries

Instructions:

1. **Preheat oven**: Preheat your oven to 350°F (175°C) and grease a loaf pan.
2. **Mix dry ingredients**: In a bowl, whisk together flour, baking powder, baking soda, and salt.
3. **Cream butter and sugar**: In another bowl, beat together butter and sugar until light and fluffy. Add the eggs, lemon zest, lemon juice, and vanilla extract, mixing well.
4. **Add dry ingredients**: Gradually add the dry ingredients, alternating with the buttermilk. Mix until just combined.
5. **Add raspberries**: Gently fold in the raspberries.
6. **Bake**: Pour the batter into the prepared loaf pan and bake for 50-60 minutes, or until a toothpick inserted comes out clean.
7. **Cool and serve**: Let the bread cool in the pan for 10 minutes, then remove from the pan and cool completely before serving.

Cranberry Orange Scones

Ingredients:

- 2 cups all-purpose flour
- 1/4 cup sugar
- 1 tbsp baking powder
- 1/2 tsp salt
- 1/2 cup cold unsalted butter, cut into small cubes
- 1/2 cup dried cranberries
- Zest of 1 orange
- 2/3 cup heavy cream
- 1 large egg
- 1 tsp vanilla extract

Instructions:

1. **Preheat oven**: Preheat your oven to 400°F (200°C) and line a baking sheet with parchment paper.
2. **Mix dry ingredients**: In a large bowl, whisk together flour, sugar, baking powder, and salt.
3. **Cut in butter**: Add cold butter cubes and cut into the flour using a pastry cutter or your fingers until the mixture resembles coarse crumbs.
4. **Add cranberries and orange zest**: Stir in dried cranberries and orange zest.
5. **Make dough**: In a separate bowl, whisk together the heavy cream, egg, and vanilla extract. Pour into the flour mixture and stir until just combined.
6. **Shape and bake**: Turn the dough onto a lightly floured surface, pat into a disk, and cut into wedges. Place the wedges on the prepared baking sheet and bake for 15-18 minutes, or until golden brown.
7. **Serve**: Cool slightly before serving, optionally drizzling with an orange glaze.

Buttermilk Biscuits with Strawberry Jam

Ingredients:

- 2 cups all-purpose flour
- 2 tsp baking powder
- 1/2 tsp baking soda
- 1/4 tsp salt
- 1/4 cup cold unsalted butter, cut into small cubes
- 3/4 cup buttermilk

Instructions:

1. **Preheat oven**: Preheat your oven to 450°F (230°C) and grease a baking sheet.
2. **Mix dry ingredients**: In a large bowl, whisk together flour, baking powder, baking soda, and salt.
3. **Cut in butter**: Add the butter and use a pastry cutter or your fingers to work it into the flour mixture until it resembles coarse crumbs.
4. **Add buttermilk**: Make a well in the center of the mixture and pour in the buttermilk. Stir gently until the dough just comes together.
5. **Shape biscuits**: Turn the dough out onto a floured surface and gently pat it into a 1-inch thick rectangle. Fold the dough in half and repeat the process to create layers. Cut out biscuits using a round cutter.
6. **Bake**: Place the biscuits on the prepared baking sheet and bake for 10-12 minutes, or until golden brown.
7. **Serve**: Serve warm with strawberry jam.

Peach and Cream Cheese Tartlets

Ingredients:

- 1 package puff pastry, thawed
- 8 oz cream cheese, softened
- 1/4 cup powdered sugar
- 1 tsp vanilla extract
- 2-3 ripe peaches, sliced thinly
- 1 tbsp honey (optional)

Instructions:

1. **Preheat oven**: Preheat your oven to 375°F (190°C) and line a baking sheet with parchment paper.
2. **Prepare the cream cheese filling**: In a small bowl, beat together the softened cream cheese, powdered sugar, and vanilla extract until smooth.
3. **Prepare the pastry**: Roll out the puff pastry and cut into 4-inch squares. Place the squares on the prepared baking sheet.
4. **Assemble the tartlets**: Spread a tablespoon of the cream cheese mixture in the center of each puff pastry square. Top with a few slices of peach.
5. **Bake**: Bake for 15-20 minutes, or until the pastry is golden and puffed.
6. **Finish and serve**: Drizzle with honey (optional) before serving. Serve warm or at room temperature.

Lemon and Thyme Tea Cookies

Ingredients:

- 2 cups all-purpose flour
- 1/2 tsp baking powder
- 1/4 tsp salt
- 1/2 cup unsalted butter, softened
- 1/2 cup sugar
- Zest of 1 lemon
- 1 tsp fresh thyme leaves
- 1 egg
- 1 tsp vanilla extract

Instructions:

1. **Preheat oven**: Preheat your oven to 350°F (175°C) and line a baking sheet with parchment paper.
2. **Mix dry ingredients**: In a bowl, whisk together flour, baking powder, and salt.
3. **Cream butter and sugar**: In another bowl, beat together butter, sugar, lemon zest, and thyme until light and fluffy.
4. **Add egg and vanilla**: Add the egg and vanilla extract, mixing well.
5. **Combine**: Gradually add the dry ingredients to the butter mixture, mixing until just combined.
6. **Shape and bake**: Roll the dough into small balls and place them on the prepared baking sheet. Flatten slightly with a fork or your fingers. Bake for 10-12 minutes, or until the edges are golden.
7. **Serve**: Let cool before serving.